Pitman New Era Shorthand Key

Anniversary Edition

Audrey O'Dea, Joan Sykes,
Julie Watson and Pamela Williams

PITMAN PUBLISHING
128 Long Acre, London WC2E 9AN

© Sir Isaac Pitman Limited 1988

First published in Great Britain 1988

British Library Cataloguing in Publication Data
Pitman New Era Shorthand Key.—
Anniversary ed.
1. Shorthand—Pitman
653′.4242   Z56.2.P5
ISBN 0 273 02901 0

Typeset, printed and bound in Great Britain
at The Bath Press, Avon

Contents

Reading and writing practice – 1

  p, p;   b, b;   p, b, p, b, p, b.
2 t, t;   d, d;   t, d, t, d, t, d.
3 ch, ch;   j, j;   ch, j, ch, j, ch, j.
  p, b, t, d, ch, j.
5 t, j, p, d, ch, b.

Reading and writing practice – 2

1 b, d; d, b; j, d; b, j.
2 d, p; t, p; ch, p; p, p.
3 ch, t; ch, d; b, t; t, t.
4 j, b; j, p; b, ch; d, j.
5 b, p; b, b; p, ch; d, t.

Reading and writing practice – 3

1 pay, day, jay.
2 date, ate, bait.
3 babe, paid, jape.
4 age, aid, ape.
5 tape, bay, page.

Reading and writing practice – 4

1 tapes
2 baits

3 dates
4 japes
5 days

Reading and writing practice – 5

1 etch
2 debt
3 jets
4 bets
5 edges

Short form and phrasing practice

1 The object is to do it, but who is to do the tapes?
2 Be his aide too.
3 Who objected to the two pages?
4 But which is the debt which is paid today?
5 It is 5 per cent per annum.

Practical dictation

1 Which date is it today?   (*5 words*)
2 The debt is paid today.   (*5 words*)
3 Pay the debts too.   (*4 words*)
4 It is his object too.   (*5 words*)
5 Which is the tape?   (*4 words*)
6 It is paid to Ted.   (*5 words*)
7 But who is to pay?   (*5 words*)
8 Which is the jet?   (*4 words*)
9 Date page two!   (*3 words*)
10 The object is to pay his debt.   (*7 words*)
11 The bet is paid!   (*4 words*)
12 Do pay the debt. Is it 5 per cent?   (*9 words*)

3 Who is to pay the debt?   (*6 words*)

4 Who objects to 5 per cent per annum to pay / the debt?   (*12 words*)

5 But it is Ted who objected!   (*6 words*)

.... *which is*

.... *pays the*

.... *bays*

.... *aid*

.... *baits*

6 .... *pep*

7 .... *page the*

8 .... *babes*

9 .... *do the*

10 .... *date the*

Curved strokes; second-place dash vowels

Reading and writing practice – 1

1 Who is to fetch the vet to the ape?
2 They say the debt is paid.
3 Fay paid the two debts.
4 Fetch the two tapes today.
5 Beth is to date the tapes today.

Reading and writing practice – 2

1 Show the photo to the vet today.
2 Who is to pay the Dutch judge?
3 It is up to us to fetch the pup.
4 Joe is to tow his boat to the bay.
5 Ted, tow the boat to the show.

Short form and phrasing practice

1 It is up to the judge to pay them.
2 Shall they have the essay to show to Joe?
3 5th February is usually the date to pay the debt.
4 They think the debt was paid today.

Practical dictation

1 Is it today they tow the boat to the bay? (*10 words*)
2 It is usual to fetch the bait today. (*8 words*)

3 Which vet is to bathe the pup?   (*7 words*)

4 Beth is to show both the tapes to the judge.   (*10 words*)

5 It is up to them to have the Boat Show / today.   (*11 words*)

6 Show them the edges which they have to sew up.   (*10 words*)

7 Pay the debt to the judge today.   (*7 words*)

8 Faith is to do the essay today.   (*7 words*)

9 They think they usually pay us to do it but / today they both say they paid Joe.   (*17 words*)

10 Which was the page they showed to us? Was it / page 2?   (*12 words*)

11 They both say they think the date was 5th February.   (*10 words*)

12 It was up to them to vote today.   (*8 words*)

13 They say they think it is the usual page which / they have to touch up. Which page have they to / do? Do they have to do both pages? (*28 words*)

14 Do they think it is the usual shape?   (*8 words*)

15 It was up to them to show the boat to / us.   (*11 words*)

Theory check

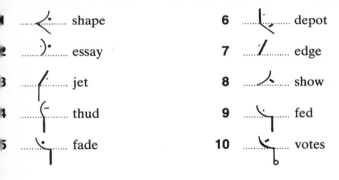

1	shape		**6**	depot	
2	essay		**7**	edge	
3	jet		**8**	show	
4	thud		**9**	fed	
5	fade		**10**	votes	

Horizontal strokes; upward strokes

Reading and writing practice – 1

1 They came today to make the change.
2 Monday, 10th February, was the day to change the name.
3 They may make enough to engage the coach.
4 They came to take the pay to the boat.
5 They objected to the gauge but it was the usual shape.

Reading and writing practice – 2

1 Monday, 17th February, was the day they came to weigh the load.
2 Do they know who it was delayed Monday's mail?
3 It may be they came to check the Yellow Pages to know the length.
4 The pages below show the way to make changes to the cheque.
5 They both say the wage cheque was unpaid.

Short form and phrasing practice

1 We have given the Mail Department the wage envelopes today.
2 Bay Mail Company Limited is to inform us today which department was usually given the cheques.
3 We shall come to give him the pay to make up the January wages today.
4 The thing is, we have never informed him who is to give the cheque to him.
5 They say the Lake Boat Company Limited may delay the load to November.

Practical dictation

1 They came to the lake today but it was too / low to bathe. (*13 words*)
2 Jake was informed today but objected to the name change. (*10 words*)
3 They will have to get to the gate to make / the jail escape. (*13 words*)
4 They came today to pay the debt they owed to / the tape company. (*13 words*)
5 We give below the thing which we think they will / have to change. (*13 words*)
6 The boat came to the bay today to load the / coal. (*11 words*)
7 Ted came up to the Toll Gate Company to pay / the debt. (*12 words*)
8 The Dutch company make the gauges but they will have / to change the name. (*14 words*)
9 Show the boat company the pale yellow envelopes. (*8 words*)
10 The gale is enough to delay the boats which came / to the gulf today. (*14 words*)
11 The mail company may think it will have to change / the way it pays the wages. (*16 words*)
12 They came to vote but we objected to the poll. (*10 words*)
13 The company cheque was delayed a month, but it was / the wages cheque we usually pay to the depot which / never came. (*22 words*)
14 The mail became delayed but we think they will locate / the yellow envelope which was given to him. (*18 words*)
15 The memo was given to the fellow who was to / load the mail. (*13 words*)

Theory check

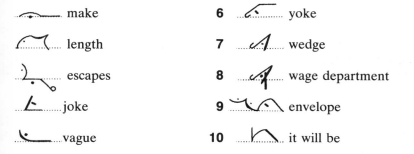

1 ⌒ make
2 ⌒ length
3 ⌒ escapes
4 ⌒ joke
5 ⌒ vague

6 ⌒ yoke
7 ⌒ wedge
8 ⌒ wage department
9 ⌒ envelope
10 ⌒ it will be

First-place vowels

1. They will take the cash to the bank at 2 today.
2. Pa paid his cheque to the bank department today.
3. They will have to take a cab to get back to the bank.
4. Give them the facts to add to the data bank.
5. Be calm. We shall manage to catch them at the bank to give them the package.

Reading and writing practice – 2

1. They bought the saw at the usual shop.
2. The autobank is among the shops at the top.
3. We have got to add 15 per cent to the cash at the bottom.
4. Attach the top page to the bottom page.
5. We have got odd jobs to do at the shop.

Short form and phrasing practice

The fact is we lack all of the cash to / pay the large debt to the bank for February. We / had to give them a cheque on the 5th February / for the January debt and the February debt is, as / we know, too large to be paid with it. It / will be unusual for the company to delay but who / will give us the cash?   (*65 words*)

1 Telephone instructions dictated to secretary by Area Sales Manager

Ask Paul for the page with the up-to-date / data for February. Attach the page for January to it. / Add them both up to give the cash for the / month and date the page at the bottom, with his / name below. Give both pages back to Paul to check. / Ask him to do the job with no delay.   (*59 words*)

2 Memo to: Shop Manager   From: Security Chief
Subject: Anticipated robbery   Date: Today's

We know they will attack the shop at 4 on / Monday, so take 95 per cent of the cash / to the bank at 2. We may manage to catch / the gang at the back of the shop with the / 5 per cent of the cash which will be given / to them. As we have informed The Law of the / attack, they will also be with us to catch the / gang.   (*71 words*)

3 Extract from the minutes of a meeting of the Board
Subject: Poor company performance

It is a shame but we may have to do / away with jobs at the company owing to lack of / cash to pay off the debts. We do have cash / owing to us but we also have a large debt / at the bank. We lack the cash for all the / back pay on the wages package but we shall have / to manage. We shall have to have long talks on / ways to change the company.   (*75 words*)

1	.... at		6	.... manage
2	.... calm		7	.... off
3	.... tall		8	.... damage
4	.... away		9	.... talk
5	.... got		10	.... knock

Third-place vowels

Reading and writing practice – 1

1 The team usually teaches on Monday.
2 They will keep the money for the big fee.
3 They had a copy of the monthly bill.
4 We shall leave them to see the mill today.
5 Teach them to attach the cheques to each bill.

Reading and writing practice – 2

1 We shall look at the big ships for the company.
2 The bank informed the youth it will mail his cheque.
3 She took the book to the lady today.
4 Look at the books and check the cash.
5 They will move the wood to the shed.

Reading and writing practice – 3

1 Keep a copy of the cheque.
2 They will be mailing the key to him.
3 Inform them it will be leaving on Monday.
4 She objected to taking the money to the Law Department.
5 They will be asking for daily copies.

Short form and phrasing practice

The young lady is going to get copies for the / company to show them the
difference in bank policy. Do / we know if we owe any money to the Law
Department? If so, it ought to be paid. We had / nothing in the bank in
January, but money is being / put in. We can go to get anything we have / at
the bank on Monday if we wish.   (*68 words*)

Confidential memo from Company Secretary to Managing Director

A change may be put into effect in February but / we have no wish to make a move. If we / can think of a different way of doing it we / shall do so. It is unusual for the Youth Party/ to delay its policy but we shall know in January / if anything is going to be different.   (*57 words*)

Memo from Chief Cashier to a new member of the department

Take the money to the bank on Monday the 5th. / The cheques can be put in the book, but the / cash ought to be put in a bag. Look at / the cheques to see if they have the date on / them. It is a big bank, which is usually busy / in the month of January.   (*55 words*)

Note from Export Manager to his secretary

We can ship the books to them in November. Attach/ a copy of the deal to the package, but mail / a copy of it to the bank. We ought also / to inform the lady in the cash department of the / deal. She has usually put the data on the page / to mail back to the company.   (*56 words*)

Theory check

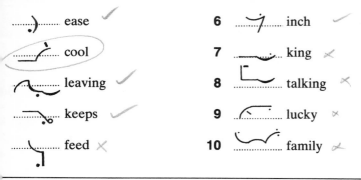

......) ...... ease ✓	**6**	......7...... inch ✓
......∕...... cool	**7**	.........,.. king ✗
∕\\...... leaving ✓	**8**	.... talking ✗
......⌐.... keeps ✓	**9**	..⌐...... lucky ✗
......\\...... feed ✗	**10**	.... family ✗

S circle; downward L

Reading and writing practice – 1

1 We may make a small loss on the two days' sales at the Boat Show.
2 It makes sense to save with a savings bank.
3 We think they will lose large sums of money at the sale on Sunday.
4 She usually leaves a message at the office if she wishes us to pay the cheques and cash into the bank.
5 Large bills and a lack of cash caused him to sell his business at a loss in January.

Reading and writing practice – 2

1 They have objected to the delay so we shall despatch the discs today.
2 The coach party of sixty ladies chose to visit the shops and have lunch in the city.
3 Take two copies of the magazine with the cash to the lady at the desk opposite the cabinets.
4 If we see James on Monday we ought to discuss the loss of jobs in the city office.
5 It is the custom for us to deposit the cash with the cheques in the bank each Wednesday.

Reading and writing practice – 3

1 We can ask him to put the small sack of money into his safe deposit box to keep it safe for us.
2 The lazy sales team was the cause of the loss of business in the Lace Department in November.
3 We know she will be busy but we shall look in at the office today.
4 It is the usual policy for the police dogs to be on show at the match.
5 The thief may make his escape if they give him enough scope to do so.

Reading and writing practice – 4

We ought to cancel the audit which was set for January and book it for February.

It will be senseless to keep on with the business, so we shall have to face the facts and put it up for sale soon, if we can.

They took the vessel on the canal but it was too large, so the pace was too slow for them.

Unless they appeal to the judge in six days they will lose the case.

We know they will object if we use only cassettes in the language lessons, so we ought to discuss it with them.

Reading and writing practice – 5

It is a long way to the village if we take the path along the edge of the lake.

We have a feeling they will succeed if they go into the film business.

If the company fails to pay the tax bill, it can seek aid at the bank.

We feel we may make a big loss on the sale of the boat unless we follow the lead given us at the Boat Show.

It is the policy of the Wages Department to inform us if the company makes any changes to the wage scale for the sales team.

Short form and phrasing practice

We have for sale several books on special subjects, especially / maths and languages, and also on government policy and business / topics. Those who wish to speak unusual languages may thus / come to us to get something. We know we can / only take so much money on these special sales but / we wish to make as much as possible. This is / because of the large bills we had to pay yesterday.   (*70 words*)

Practical dictation

1 Memo regarding an enquiry for special lace

The special lace for which the lady asks is sold / in the city shops to mak‹
wedding veils. If she / wishes to have a length of it she will have / to giv‹
us full details of the width and shade, / which we shall pass on to th‹
shop. Only so / much of this lace can be bought each month because / i
takes so long to make.   (*66 words*)

2 Report about an order from a business agency

Miss James, who has the business agency in the village, / came into th‹
shop several days ago. She paid for / two dozen yellow pencils along wit‹
a box of large / envelopes. She wishes us to despatch these to the
agency / in the village. We ought to put a copy of / the bill in the packag‹
At the agency she also / teaches many subjects useful to anybody wh‹
wishes to succeed / in the office skills exams. They come into the shop
to get things too.   (*84 words*)

3 Memo to Despatch Department

Take the case of cassettes with the discs to the / docks on Wednesday t‹
stow them in the space which / is put at this company's disposal. Becaus‹
they use special / loading techniques at these docks, the Dutch compan‹
vetoes the / use of nails in the lids. Check the ship is / set to sail on
Monday. Make up the bill which / is to be paid this month and mail it to‹
the company's office in Canada.   (*75 words*)

Theory check

1	looks	6	falling
2	envelopes	7	vale
3	justice	8	valley
4	safely	9	skills
5	succeeds	10	speaks

Reading and writing practice – 1

The remedy for the company's loss was to remove the ore.
They had to make room for the firm's car.
This month Eric has sold his shares in the tour company.
Early in January they had to go to a wedding in Rome.
They had to erase the name of the firm on the airmail envelope.

Reading and writing practice – 2

The lady rang the firm's large factory to ask to borrow a pair of tow ropes
for the red car.
They came early to remove the red rug and took it to the back door for
loading on the lorry.
It was a rush to get things ready for the pair, who will marry in Rome in
January.
The large ridge at Red Gap appears to be rich in ore, so the firm wishes
to take a fair share.
Owing to the severe injury to the young lad's arm, the firm had to
remedy the safety catch on the car door.

Reading and writing practice – 3

We shall urge the authority to engage a lawyer so as to remove any fear
or alarm they may have.
The charge for the upstairs room with a veranda was fair but the visitor
had to have a garage for his car.
The officer's answer was sincere but the charge for the repair to the rare
object appears to be an error.
In March the company lawyer had given him authority to carry on with
his career in a different firm.
The officer assures us we can park the car on the shore if we go to see the
marina tomorrow.

Short form and phrasing practice

We wish to give our sincere thanks to those who / came along to our charity sale early this year. What / we receive in this way goes to relieve, as far / as possible, the despair of many poor and needy families. / We are making arrangements to have a rummage-sale in / aid of our charity in March, for which we shall / require a large room. We should wish to know as / early as possible if your firm can spare a room / for two hours which will be satisfactory for this purpose. (*90 words*)

Practical dictation

1 Footwear shop seasonal sale

Our Sale this year is for four days only so / we urge our customers to come along to our shop, / which is in Rock Road. We ensure our customers get / a fair deal and our level of service never varies. / We are selling things at exceedingly low rates because we / have to make room for a full range of shoes / and boots in all colours which we have bought ready / for the autumn season. Come in tomorrow and get yourself / pair — or several pairs. (*85 words*)

2 Memo to: Site Foreman   From: Works Manager
Subject: Removal of refuse   Date: Today's

The load of rubbish at the rear of the factory / makes us uneasy and we are sorry to say we / have no authority to make the guilty party remove it. / It will be a relief if they will remedy this / but, as the rubbish appears to be going to spill / on to our territory, we should make arrangements to move / it in our lorries. We shall urge our lawyers to check a similar case in which a large firm was / required to remove a load of earth which it had / put in a narrow road and which may have led / to injury to visitors to the factory. (*107 words*)

3 Car servicing advertisement

In the early months of the year, especially in January / and February, garages are busy with repairs to cars and / lorries. They all have something wrong with them which has / required taking each right of the road — and yours may / be among them! We are a firm which can give / a door-to-door service if required and which will / charge a fair rate for repairs. We carry spares for / many different makes of car and it is our policy / to give a speedy service, which comes with our guarantee. / Give us a ring today!   (*95 words*)

.... charge

6 .... deter

.... repair

7 .... beware

.... salary

8 .... arrears

.... cashier

9 .... censor

.... erratic

10 .... we shall arrange

Diphthongs, triphones and diphones

Reading and writing practice – 1

1 Do we have a fire sign in the office to say what to do if the alarm goes off?
2 We have a lengthy invoice to type which should be ready for mailing by 5 tonight.
3 By the time we arrive at the sale they will have sold the china cups we like.
4 It will be a shame if she retires since we enjoy the things she writes so much.
5 What advice can we give on the use of the data bank to remedy this type of error at source?

Reading and writing practice – 2

1 For a small cash outlay we can buy the factory.
2 Rubik's Cube was a toy with six sides — popular with the youth of some years ago.
3 They will announce the monetary failure of the company in time to catch the news tonight.
4 The rooms they occupy have a layout to face the south of the city.
5 They chose a poor site for the beauty shop — it was asking for failure.

Reading and writing practice – 3

1 The object of the share issue is to raise new revenue for the company.
2 The oil company may have to review its policies in view of the news given out by the authorities today.
3 Few of the items are of any monetary value to us now.
4 They will announce the issue of the shares in a few days' time.
5 It is time to renew the lease on the office we occupy in New Avenue.

Reading and writing practice – 4

We wish to book a large berth with a shower for the voyage.
We are given a mileage allowance on top of our salaries for the use of our cars.
They think they will be buying some of the shares we are issuing.
A wide variety of life annuities can be bought today for a low outlay.
Go via the road to the south. This adds fewer miles to the route.

Reading and writing practice – 5

It seems his business failure was the cause of his suicide.
It is no use sighing! The job has to be carried out tomorrow.
We are suing the company for the damage due to the leakage of oil into the sewers.
We have tenuous links with the Science Department. We can ask them to carry out some research for us into the side-effects.
We have no reason to see this as a joyous affair. We are basing our views on silly and fatuous advice given by those who know few of the facts and who are out of date.

Reading and writing practice – 6

Go to the photocopier and take five copies for the senior sales team. Have them ready by tonight.
We are following up your idea of showing videos in our shops in view of your theory it will aid sales.
The shares are showing a loss and it may be ruinous for the company if this carries on.
Summarise your ideas for changing the layout of the audio area.
It is obvious she is serious but we have no time to talk right now.

Short form and phrasing practice

should like to discuss my tax affairs with you, / and I write to ask you to ive me two / dates when I may come to see you. I wish / to have advice as to why my tax bill is / now so much. The reasons are beyond me. Can you give me a choice of times, if possible outside the / period 10 am to 4 pm, and I / will say which suits me. How do you usually charge? / Is it by the hour or have you a set / fee for your attention to my tax affairs?   (*98 words*)

Practical dictation

1   Letter to travellers about surcharge on holiday

I am sorry to have to write to you to / advise of a 10 per cent surcharge which will appear / on the invoice for your voyage to the South China Sea on which you are due to leave in 5 / months' time. This is because of a rise in oil / charges which we are having to pass on to you / . I apologise for this, but we have had no choice.   (*70 words*)

2   Extract from a financial report on share speculation

The 5 per cent rise in the value of the / shares since the issue 10 months ago was really of / no use to us since we had bought them with / a view to making a killing. The cause of the / failure of our idea was the poor sale in the / 4 months following May, which had an effect on the / share value. On the advice of the bank we shall / now sell.   (*72 words*)

3   Memo to: Security Officer   From: Construction Manager
Subject: Investigation into   Date: Today's
site accident

Owing to the failure of the safety policy of our / company, we have a boy with a serious injury. It / is our duty to look into this thoroughly. I wish to have the following facts when you know them:
1 /   Why was the boy on the site and at what / time?
2   What signs had security put by the side / of the sewer?
3   How wide was the sewer and / what was the depth?
4   Was the gate to the / site secure at the time?
5   What changes ought we / to make to our safety policy to reassure the authorities / of our ability to manage the sites safely?   (*108 words*)

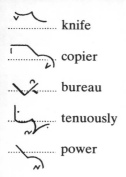 knife

.... copier

.... bureau

.... tenuously

.... power

6 .... various

7 .... loyal

8 .... county

9 .... eyes

10 .... earlier

Consonant H

Reading and writing practice – 1

1 My house is too far away so I shall go by car.
2 The load was too heavy for the lorry to go on the ferry.
3 I shall see the head of our Sales Department at the showroom tomorrow.
4 I shall hurry to the hotel ahead of the party to deal hastily with the meal arrangements.
5 I hope the head of your department can give us the full history of the house.

Reading and writing practice – 2

1 He spoke to the customer for a long time at the hotel.
2 He should know the Highway Code thoroughly to pass the exam.
3 How high a fee may we charge in the museum?
4 The firm said it will charge higher rates for the service.
5 The hike they arranged in January was a failure owing to the heavy snowfall.

Reading and writing practice – 3

1 Miss Hall can have a room in the new hostel at the top of the hill.
2 The huge house should make an ideal home for the large family.
3 The new judge may hear the case put by the lawyer for our company today.
4 He knew the whole history of her case and put it to the officer in charge.
5 We wish to visit your health farm with a view to booking a holiday for six in July.

The mishap on the ship was due to the failure of the safety locks on the heavy doors.

It will be an uphill task to secure the business deal as the hire company is unhappy with the new arrangements.

My company wishes to buy her leasehold house and shop but I know she hopes to keep them for many years to come.

Short form and phrasing practice

hope the manufacturer can arrange early despatch of the / tapes manufactured yesterday. If he will mail the invoice to / the head office of ur Society, they will pay by / cheque. In the meantime it would be a help / we knew whose tapes we can use on Monday. (*49 words*)

Practical dictation

Letter to a publisher

I wish to buy some back copies of two of / your magazines. They are 'Health in the Home' and 'The / History of the House'. I should like to buy the / January, February and March issues of each of these, if / you have them. (*43 words*)

Memo to sales representative from Sales Manager

Thank you for your help. I know the head of / the firm which manufactures the hacksaws; his name is Harry / Hill. I am informed he is on holiday now but / I shall see him in a month's time when he / arrives home. It is handy having such a firm in / our housing area. I think he will be happy to / give us 5 per cent off his invoice for cash. (*70 words*)

Letter to a local estate agent

The July issue of 'Highroad and Highway', which will be / on sale on Tuesday, gives the history of Hope Road / on which you live. I shall be

happy to hear / your views on the new homes in Hope Road. Each /
house has garage space for two cars and also a / large lounge, but we
have had them on our books / for sale for some time now. We think the
valuer / has put too high a value on these leasehold homes. / In fact we
are informed they will sell for far / less.   (*91 words*)

Theory check

1 .... heavy

2 .... heading

3 .... hang

4 .... hoax

5 .... hectic

6 .... mahogany

7 .... harm

8 .... help

9 .... whom

10 .... livelihood

Reading and writing practice – 1

I suggest you check our itemised list of stock, which must be up to date.
The cost of waste in this company last August was just too high.
All staff must take the tests for the new posts if we are to select the best.
I am suggesting the adjusting of the statistics to show the real state of affairs.
A status check allows you to see if the storage space on the disc is used up.

Reading and writing practice – 2

I have a host of suggestions for making our posters artistic.
Administer the fixed dose twice a day and he will get relief much faster.
A rise of 5 per cent per annum should make the investors happy but what of the borrowers?
'Master Investor' is the name we shall give to our new range of policies.
Check to see if his name is on the register as having large, unpaid debts.

Reading and writing practice – 3

Taxes are necessary if a society chooses to help the poor successfully.
If he passes his exams, I shall insist he carries on with his studies.
Daily exercises are a necessity if we are to stay healthy.
We still have no idea of the causes of the excessive losses which the company faces.
I am sorry to lose your services but wish you success in your new post.

Reading and writing practice – 4

1 The polls show a huge swing to the right in the vote.
2 I swear I had nothing to do with stealing the money.
3 Look for the switch on the right by the swing door and switch it off
4 They will be swayed by your talk of success and vote for us.
5 I would go for a swim in the sea but the swelling on my wrist is still sor

Short form and phrasing practice

As we have a ready sale in this city for / our items, I think we can influenc
the buyers of / most of the largest companies in as much as we / can mak
them see how much they will save if / they stay with us. As well as bein
influenced themselves, / though, they will wish to see if we can influenc
the smaller companies to buy our manufactures. I shall speak / to our Are
Sales Managers first, next Monday morning at / 9 am, as is my custom, an
inform them, / as far as possible, of what we have in store. / Although it
usual for each Area Sales Manager himself / to do so, I will speak to ou
sales force / myself on this subject as soon as possible. When I / have th
authority and also know it is all right / to make the necessary arrangement
we can go ahead. Our / Market Research office is as usual doing a mailin
next / month to almost all the largest customers.   (*167 words*)

Practical dictation

1 Memo to: All Staff   From: WP Supervisor
Subject: File codifying   Date: Today's

If we are to use our storage media successfully, all / staff must nam
files just as discussed in the company / manual. Sloppy coding leads t
waste of time for the / department's staff and, in some excessive case
lost data for / staff managers. As we are aiming to speed up the / acces
time for all files as much as possible, we / ask you to help us by doir
this. Thank you.   (*70 words*)

Extract from an article on the value of exercise

Nowadays it is usual for both sexes to take some / form of exercise. Some pay for the services of a / gym itself and this is fixed by the hour or / on an annual basis. In some cases the idea is / to shed the excess stones and reduce the waist size / as fast as you can, but for those already in / shape the aim is just to test the body as / far as possible by honest exercising. All advisory bodies on / health always emphasize the value of daily exercise.   (*88 words*)

Letter regarding appointment of Research Manager

We are happy to inform you of your success in / being given the new post of Research Manager. Since it / will be necessary for you to have skill in using / the vast data banks held here by ourselves to access / statistics as soon as possible, we suggest you take up / your post on 1st August. As we know you are / used to different data banks, at first the ancillary staff / in the department are to assist you to adjust, and / thus to master the differences faster. We hope these suggestions / are satisfactory for you and we hope to receive your / answer soon. (*102 words*)

Theory check

.... stereo

.... elastic

.... offices

.... statistics

.... refused

6 .... Swiss

7 .... necessary

8 .... barrister

9 .... cassette

10 .... pasta

Halving

Reading and writing practice – 1

1 We marked and checked the notes which had to go in the guide-book
2 The bad debt had reached a large sum and it was thought best not to le them have anything else.
3 The guide in the museum stopped and talked to us and showed us th sort of things used to light the homes of those who lived long ago.
4 I shall be happy if you will let me know if you can meet me when I ge to your city by the late jet.
5 The tights and stockings showed some slight faults and we hoped we might get them changed on the spot.

Reading and writing practice – 2

1 We have not yet received the report which you stated would be issuee yesterday morning.
2 The leaflets and booklets, along with the tickets, have not yet arrive for our holiday in the Far East.
3 We have no doubt the estimate for the system to heat the new hospita is to be submitted when the site managers meet next month.
4 The actual method specified in the expert's report is fully guaranteee
5 They will no doubt notify us of the exact limits to be reached when th new estate is built.

Reading and writing practice – 3

1 The detailed evidence seemed to indicate the Board should take step to secure the necessary capital required to get the desired result.
2 The boy, who had insured his old car until the end of the month, hear of a different scheme which would undoubtedly save him money.
3 He filled in the necessary card and mailed it on the 21st to the compan named on the attached leaflet.

It appeared to him he had made a good choice and he was assured of at least a moderate yield on his capital by the middle of the year.

The report was delayed until the 23rd for a skilled estimate but when the detached cottage was valued they decided the money would have to be borrowed.

eading and writing practice – 4

It seemed a pity they chose to locate the hotel on the busy route to the capital.

The fact is we liked the effect of the special lighting which was designed for the hat department window.

We hope to select the right candidate for the vacant post this morning.

At the height of the export boom, shares rose by the minute at a rapid rate.

The agenda was dictated by the office manager and dated 1st August.

hort form and phrasing practice

e are sorry to hear that for some time now / the hand-operated lathe you ught at our factory has / failed to satisfy your requirements. We have had vord / with our marketing manager following your enquiry, and he quite / cepts that under our manufacturer's guarantee goods can be sent / back thout charge if they have failed at some time / to do the job specified. is would appear to be / so in your case. As you stated that you wished / have your money refunded and paid in at the / National Bank, this could arranged if it is possible / for you to let us have your sales certificate mediately. / Let us know if you decide you wish the money / to be paid t to you instead. (*127 words*)

ractical dictation

The Works Manager leaves a message for his secretary

I think it is a good idea to get up- / to-date catalogues and leaflets as soon as possible about / automatic heating systems for the new factory which is to / be built on the outskirts of the estate. When these / are received I would like you to set out in / a few words a summary of the benefits of the / different systems with detailed supporting evidence relating to the varying / aspects. Following this, we would invite estimates of cost and, / at the same time, get a forecast of when the goods could be installed if we decided to go ahead. / Could you have this carried out ready for when I / get back on Wednesday? Thank you. (*116 words*)

2 Factory Manager's Report

The factory manager, in a report submitted to the Board, / noted the most satisfactory results appeared to be indicated for / the year under review. He felt that they would be / delighted that, because of the healthy state of national affairs, / both home and export markets have enjoyed good sales, as / could be seen on the sheet attached to the agenda. / An entirely new policy was operating which ensured that the / Sales Department could be relied on to give immediate attention to any bad debts which might have existed in the / past. All those customers who remitted without delay could be / given an allowance 5 per cent. The report was / accepted and adopted by the Board. (*116 words*)

3 Memo to: All Staff   From: Managing Director
Subject: New packaging   Date: Today's

We have lately decided that it is time we looked / into all aspects of our methods of packaging goods. Our / packets are apt to appear outdated to our customers and / we intend to select an absolutely new range packaging / designed to meet the needs of today.

To this end, / we are going to launch an intensive pilot scheme in the next fortnight in which it is hoped our staff / may participate, and a start be asked to submit / designs for our medium-sized range of goods. These should / be smart and yet be made to our budget. We shall make an award for the best design submitted.   (*109 words*)

Theory check

1	`(⁻` thought		6	`⌄` writing
2	`⟋⟍` report		7	`ᵛ⌐` dynamite
3	`⌐` moved		8	`⌐` married
4	`⌐ₒ` assumed		9	`6⌐` solid
5	`⟨` thousand		10	`ᵧ` if it is

Reading and writing practice – 1

The price of goods increased in the months of October and November but fell in March and April.

The name and address of the manager of the new branch was put in the company's database.

If it is possible the teacher would like the progress charts by Tuesday.

The trial had to be cancelled. It will be delayed for some time.

The young teacher's thesis was so successful that he was asked to present it to a group of graduates.

Reading and writing practice – 2

The secretary arranged for the company's stickers to be sent to all branches.

He is a leader of industry but I disagree with his extreme policy.

We have no doubt that the new district manager has decided to express his views in the next sales report.

It will be necessary to describe the items set out in the industrial booklet.

An extra secretary was required for the purpose of dealing with the increased price proposals agreed by the company.

Reading and writing practice – 3

I regret to inform you that the girl has not paid for the course of lectures this term.

The sales manager said that he had ordered the carpet in a darker shade of grey.

They came directly they heard the secretary had the target figures ready.

4 With regard to the property purchased in April, our records show t
a survey was carried out.

5 Directly you have made each sale, record the price, parcel up the go
and tie them with string.

Short form and phrasing practice – 1

Dear Dr Price

My secretary said you had met in / the street, but unfortunately she v
not at liberty to / give you a description of the projected new courses. Sl
said you appeared to be surprised by this, but the / truth is that the cou
leaflets have still to be / numbered and printed. The Principal is maki
arrangements for a / member of staff to number each leaflet during th
next / few days and the leaflets should be printed by the / end of the mon

I remember that some time ago / you asked about our principles an
methods of care and, / as these are set out in the larger booklet, my /
secretary has made a note to send you a copy. /

You will be delighted to know that the Chair of / the new departmen
to go to Doctor Straight, and / I am certain this will come as no surprise t
you. He said he remembered you and sent his regards. /

Yours sincerely   (*162 words*)

Reading and writing practice – 4

1 He offered to send the freight on the ship but it was delayed goin§
through Customs.

2 She was offered either a free book or voucher by the Market Resea
Manager to take part in the survey.

3 He looked through the report the other day.

4 He offered to send the freight on Friday, but said he would try to ge
to us sooner if possible.

5 The secretary started to type the average sales figures for October
directly she arrived at the office.

Before the freight is despatched on Thursday, a list of those items being sent free of charge should be entered in the database.
The banker offered to look through the records on Friday to alleviate the pressure on the office staff.
The chart showed the summer figures; on Friday the average yearly figures are to be sent.
Did the district officer discover fresh evidence?
The freight cases have a description and number on them.

Short form and phrasing practice – 2

ccording to our Sales Manager, it is possible to increase / sales of our roducts. However, in our view it may / not be easy to sell some of our isure goods / in all parts of the target area. I can assure / you that our Iarket Research Manager, Mr Bright, is looking / into the progress made ɔ far. It appears from recent / newspaper reports that resorts near the sea re very popular / for short breaks. This could, of course, lead to icreased / sales of our 'Water Pleasure' goods. It is necessary to / be sure ʌat these newspaper remarks are true, so I / have asked Mr Bright to ɔsearch the facts and to / come over tomorrow. Now that he has moved he / only a mere three miles away, which makes it very / easy for us to meet ɔ discuss tactics.   (*138 words*)

Practical dictation

Letter from an estate agent

Dear Mr Pride
    Thank you for asking this firm to / handle the sale of your property. So far we have / measured the site and room sizes. We have had a / description typed and stickers pasted in our showcase. Straightaway my / secretary sent the details to a banker, who is moving / to a branch in this district and who has expressed / the wish to purchase a property similar to yours. In / our view it appears that your property may be right / for him.

We anticipate an early sale of your property / and would like you
let us know which day / in April you hope to move out of the house.
Yours sincerely   (*112 words*)

2   Letter about a new range of goods for sale

Dear Sir
Our industry is extremely eager to produce the / type of goods
needed by business firms for office use. / Until now we have produce
only a limited range of / fixtures and fittings in four basic colours.
However, it is / possible for us now to offer an extra range of / goo
and a description of our proposed new spring range / of goods is se
for your perusal. We would ask / you to study this carefully and to fill i
the / attached form, which gives you scope to express your views / as
what business managers are seeking.
Thank you for / your time in filling in this short market research
form. /
Yours faithfully
Market Research Manager   (*115 words*)

3   Letter from a freight transport company

Dear Sirs
As you already know, in all parts of / the industry freight costs hav
increased rapidly during the past / few years. We are an expert carria
company offering very / reduced rates to all parts of Europe and speci
package / deals to the Far East. Free estimates are given for / all oth
trips. Express rates can be offered too.
I / can assure you that our service is fast and we / can handle bot
your fragile and heavy goods. Our team / of packers can be used if
required.
I am sure / that you are aware of the fact that our service / is alrea
widely used by other large firms in your / district. However, if you
would like our Sales Manager to / visit you to describe our terms in ful
it will / give me pleasure to make arrangements for him to do / so.
Yours faithfully
Freight Carriage Ltd   (*146 words*)

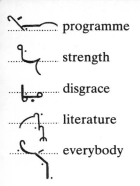 programme

 strength

 disgrace

 literature

 everybody

6 .... forgot

7 .... conquer

8 .... street

9 .... direct

10 .... attorney

Reading and writing practice – 1

1 The salesman said he would show the new machine to the factory manager.
2 She was given a loan at 10 per cent per annum and it was arranged th that it should be repaid by the end of the year.
3 It was his turn to return the monthly bulletin to the staff library.
4 Everyone can earn more money if they begin the overtime in June
5 The man had forgotten that everyone had arranged to remain in th office to key in the data.

Reading and writing practice – 2

1 The salesman and his colleague attended the training course.
2 The assistant dealt with the correspondence about the merchandise which was due for shipment in June.
3 The manager wanted to extend his skills so he attended a course to learn word processing.
4 Our site is on the western side of the town, and the demand for on-si training courses has increased there.
5 A proposal was made, and this was seconded and carried, to increa the number of shipments.

Reading and writing practice – 3

1 The students live some distance from the training course.
2 It was against the bank's policy to allow large loans without collater:
3 He finds the monthly payments are too much for him to make.
4 It remains to be seen if the day's events lead to extra business but hope to find demand for our products increasing.
5 The expense accounts must be submitted in June if payments are to made in August.

he factory owner felt that new machinery would be expensive / but in his
pinion it was necessary if output was / to be increased. He organised the
xpenditure and informed the / foreman that the machines would arrive
ithin the next few / days. The foreman stressed that there would be
enerally some / delays in manufacture when the change-over was going
n, / as the men would have to get used to the / new machines. However,
e knew that in the long term / these would be much better than the old
nes. He / asked if all of his men could have their own / copy of the
achine training manual, and the owner said / that this had been arranged.
he owner would be going / to visit the northern and southern area offices
nd asked / the foreman to let him know if the machines had / not been
eceived by Thursday next.   (*146 words*)

Letter to Personnel Manager regarding work experience placements

Dear Mr Green

Thank you for agreeing to take two / secretarial students on office
experience for the month of June / in your southern export office.

The students are following a / course in shorthand, audio,
background to business, office management and / word processing. If
required, they can produce typewritten scripts. They / are also studying
German. Both students are looking forward to / their office experience
and I am asking them to send / you copies of the course details with
their own current / course grades.

The students do not have a car but / I think arrangements are being
made by your secretary for / them to be given permits to use your staff
coach. /

Yours sincerely

Course Teacher   (*114 words*)

Memorandum to Reprographics Manager

As you know, on Wednesday next our own office bulletin / is to be
printed. A design for the layout has / already been sent to you but the
cover design is / too expensive and the accounts department did not
pass it / for payment. If you will return the cover to me, / I will amend it
and send a corrected one to / you as soon as possible. This new bulletin
has been / organised by the junior staff and it is to give / details of all
events arranged by them. I had not / planned to make a charge for

it, and as a / free bulletin I feel it will be very popular. I / did 'phon
you earlier today but found you out of / your office and I am not ir
tomorrow. I understand / that you will not be in the office again until
Monday next and so I cannot discuss this with you / in person.
(*152 words*)

3 Letter about the opening of a new factory

Dear Mr Brown

Because of increased demand for our machine / parts from all ove
the country in the last three / years, our former factory and staff ha
experienced overloading and / stress. However, we are now happy t
announce the opening / of our new factory on the Northern Industri&
Estate. We / can not only make routine machine parts there, but we
also have a repair and servicing bay. A new service / we can offer is fre
estimates for custom-made machine / parts from your own design
patterns. Measurements, of course, need / to be absolutely accurate
and, if you are not sure / about these and require assistance, our
salesmen can help you. /

You will shortly be receiving more correspondence from us,
together / with our brochure showing full details of our services and
our new factory. We are having an Open Evening on / Wednesday
next, and two Open Days in June when we / hope you and your
General Manager may be at liberty / to attend our factory tour and
short lecture.

Yours sincerely /
John Green
Machine Parts Ltd   (*175 words*)

Theory check

1	.... known	6	.... spending
2	.... drawn	7	.... country
3	.... movement	8	.... stands
4	.... current	9	.... fenced
5	.... extended	10	.... lines

Reading and writing practice – 1

We went on a tour of the West Country but everywhere the weather was wet and windy.

Wherever we went we could hear the howling of the wind, which kept us awake at night.

If you are not going to let us have the lengths of wood we want by Wednesday, we shall have to get them elsewhere.

The whitewood furniture was brought to the house by Mr White.

Once more we heard the whistle of the railway train somewhere in the distance.

Reading and writing practice – 2

We sent the work to you five weeks ago and we are worried that you may not have it ready in time.

We are aware that the work did not warrant the goods remaining in our warehouse for any length of time.

The warden of the youth hostel warned the group of walkers to tread warily on the forest footpaths.

The woman was very weary as a result of her long walk in the warm weather and it was not easy to awaken her the following morning.

Most of the company's wagons are out of warranty and we are aware that the worst of them could not be worth very much.

Reading and writing practice – 3

The wealthy businessman was well known for the attention he paid to the welfare and well-being of his workforce.

The Western Waterworks Company managers were worried that the weather would not be warm enough to attract the crowds to their annual Open Day at the reservoir.

3　Whilst the dealers were unwilling at first to let us have the necessar woodwork for the window frames, they subsequently released some from the warehouse.

4　Meanwhile we rely on your goodwill to send us as soon as possible tl wheels we ordered from you some weeks ago.

5　Will you kindly let us know the whereabouts of the wire egg whisk: which appear to have gone astray in transit.

Short form and phrasing practice

At the beginning of the month some share prices on / stock exchanges throughout the world showed an altogether worthwhile gain. / The mu respected former university lecturer, who now practises as / a broker in tl city, predicted that industrials would remain / strong and should do ver well for the next three / weeks. However, he expects that the insuranc market will not / hold up, and will tend to lose ground this week, / togeth with many property shares which were over-priced. He / doubted wheth the average person was familiar with the workings / of the Stock Exchang or made any inspection of share / prices.　(*101 words*)

Practical dictation

1　Letter of enquiry

Dear Sirs

Will you kindly let us have as soon / as possible your best price f the hardware listed on / the attached work sheet. We should also lil your advice / as to whether it will be worth while for us / to take o insurance on the more expensive goods while / they are in transit. Tl wire baskets and wheeled trolleys / are intended for use in supermarkets and we expect we / shall want somewhere in the regi of five thousand of / each of these items. We expect the goods will b sent by your wagon, as usual, to our works within / the next three weeks.

Yours faithfully
Purchasing Manager　(*108 words*)

Reply to letter of enquiry

Dear Sirs

We have pleasure in sending you herewith our / current price list for the goods you specified on your / work sheet. Our products are respected everywhere and we frequently / export our goods to many countries throughout the world. You / will not be worried by the wheels on the supermarket / trolleys locking as sometimes happens with those made by other / manufacturers. This is because we practise only the best methods / of manufacture and the parts making up our wire trolleys / are welded together for extra strength. You are invited to / carry out an inspection of the goods before you buy / and we know very well that you will not be / disappointed if you purchase our products, which come with a / full warranty.

Yours faithfully

Sales Manager   (*126 words*)

Extract from newspaper article

Women barristers have been heard to remark that the horsehair / wigs which they are required to wear in court are / too warm, especially in hot weather, and spoil a hairstyle / too! However, there are those who assert that wigs add / somewhat to the air of dignity and respect in court / whilst at the same time they enhance the well-dressed / woman barrister's appearance. This is especially true of the film / industry and actresses are more than happy to appear in / lawyer's gown and wig. Whilst many women undoubtedly find them / annoying, wigs are likely to be worn in British courts / for many years to come.   (*105 words*)

Theory check

✎ where	6	✎ meanwhile
✎ warehouse	7	✎ framework
✎ weaken	8	✎ who were not
✎ warm	9	✎ 6 weeks
✎ unwell	10	✎ aware

L Hook

Reading and writing practice – 1

1 We plan to meet in the classroom at nine o'clock to enable us to plac[e]
all the available plans on the table.
2 Some employers in the glass bottle industry and in the local glue factor[y]
have had labour problems in the past year.
3 We shall be glad to replace all the valuable articles stolen from the
cycle club.
4 The play is based on a simple story and is entitled 'The Blue Table'[.]
5 The local suppliers disclosed that they were able to replace all the
exclusive display items of glassware which they had supplied in Apri[l]

Reading and writing practice – 2

1 The result of the match was decided by his powerful kick which score[d]
the penalty in the final minute of the game.
2 On their arrival the developers had insisted on the removal of the
beautiful flower garden.
3 The traveller finally opened his black case and produced a sample o[f]
the flasks he was selling.
4 As the flood water flowed into the flat and covered the floor, the fami[ly]
fled from their home.
5 The fact that a powerful member of his Legal Department could pas[s]
secrets to the enemy so effectively, baffled the Head of the Civil
Service.

Reading and writing practice – 3

1 He personally supervised the arrival of the loads of gravel at the site[.]
2 The officer ordered the removal of the flag on his arrival at the
barracks.

The author revelled in the news that his novel had been received with such acclaim.

Because of the heavy influx of goods at the rail terminal, all holiday leave was cancelled.

The naval officer was grateful that he had been chosen to take part in the nautical display.

Reading and writing practice – 4

It is essential that you return the official document personally as early as possible.

In a solicitor's office, where law is the speciality, the shelves will be filled to capacity with legal books.

The doctor placed the girl's name on the register of partially-sighted persons.

Many high-class florists now find that the sale of artificial flowers forms an essential part of their business.

The football fans of the away team were marshalled by the police from the rail terminal to the sports ground to avoid any trouble.

Reading and writing practice – 5

I know the employees will meet the challenge set by the manufacturers and will double the current sales.

The student made a final visit to the college to collect his certificate.

On Polling Day it was necessary for the Presiding Officer to delegate some of his duties to the clerks.

The staff were asked to tolerate the party of young children during their tour of the firm.

Candidates from both political parties spoke to the pupils of the local sixth form college.

Short form and phrasing practice

Thank you for the statement which was delivered yesterday. I / must, however, dispute the balance shown. The amounts credited to / my account

are made up largely of salary payments but / other sundry items are al
included, and I believe one / or two of these items may be incorrect. Th
can / be distinguished by the different code numbers shown beside them
Nevertheless when I called your office this morning your assistant / refus
to tell me anything regarding my account. Equally, it / is remarkable tha
is increasingly hard for people to / obtain details of their accounts over t
'phone. You must / realise I am unable to call at the bank during / norn
working hours. I believed when I opened my account / that it would not
necessary for me to come / to the building itself, especially in the cold
weather. *(139 words)*

Practical dictation

1 Letter regarding a home for the disabled

Dear Sir

It is clear that we shall not be / able to meet this month if the
problems with the / building are not settled soon. The local author
claims that / the place is unsuitable for use as a home for / the disable

Nevertheless, it is my belief that with the / valuable assistance of c
Civil Engineer and Clerk of Works / we shall be able to develop a
number of specially- / designed residential flats.

I shall be grateful if you will / let me have the plans as early as
possible to / enable me to make the necessary approaches.

Yours faithfully *(99 words)*

2 Letter from an insurance company following a burglary

Dear Madam

I was very sorry to receive your message / this morning reportin
burglary at your home last night. / I shall be pleased if you will fill
the / enclosed claims form showing the date and approximate time o
the break-in and when it was discovered.

I note / that although you had checked the security system befo
leaving, / the burglar managed to climb into the house by breaking ,
double-glazed window. I believe many valuable personal articles / we
stolen. Please include each item in the form. We / hope to be able
settle your claim as soon / as possible.

Yours faithfully *(104 words)*

A reply to an enquiry regarding floor tiles

Dear Sir

I enclose our latest pamphlet which includes our / full range of floor tiles. As you know, we originally / supplied plain black tiles only, but now we produce them / in a beautiful blue and a bright flame colour. We / also manufacture a special glazed type which is coated with / a clear varnish.

We have recently experienced some labour troubles / but these problems have been finally settled. We can supply / immediate part delivery from stock, the balance being despatched in / one month's time.

I shall be pleased to receive your / reply and our specialist staff will be available to see / you at all times.

Yours faithfully   (*106 words*)

F/V Hook

Reading and writing practice – 1

1 I think we need a more active sales drive if we are to be more effecti▮ in the spring.
2 I will speak to you with the chief buyer in half an hour's time over ▮ coffee.
3 The development team has some rough ideas which may well lead ▮ the success we deserve.
4 Hold some money in reserve until I approve of its withdrawal.
5 The solicitor's brief says it will be tough but feels we have enough pro▮ to present an effective case.

Reading and writing practice – 2

1 A draft copy is a rough copy which is amended and approved for t▮ final copy.
2 Coffee will be served in the lounge which has been reserved for half ▮ hour.
3 Draft a brief circular and I will have it approved tomorrow.
4 It is not good to drift along in a job and then find you have achieve▮ nothing.
5 I observed all the amendments you made to the draft and we achieve▮ the success we deserved in the end.

Reading and writing practice – 3

1 I refer to your recent telephone call regarding the above and divide m▮ response into two parts, as shown below.
2 Relative to last year's profits, this year's profits are up by 15 per cen▮
3 The bank will definitely give me a personal advance subject to proof ▮ my salary.

I have the perfect plan to secure even bigger profits for the company.
I prefer coffee to tea provided that it is not too strong when it is served.

The graphs for the April figures can be seen on graphics terminal three.
Recall standard paragraphs three, six and nine, and give me a
print-out to approve.
She generally takes all the photographs of the models in advance of the
season and approves the best for the magazine articles.
He approves of dividing the profits as this serves to give an incentive to
employees.
Wives and husbands are the only relatives to be allowed in for the
private viewing.

Short form and phrasing practice

spite of a third notice, you have neglected to / make any payment on
ur mortgage in the last four / months. You ought to have tried to pay at
ast / some part of the amount owing. It would appear that / you have
fficulty with your financial arrangements. You may call / to see me on
iday afternoon or, if this is / difficult, I respectfully suggest that instead
this a representative / of the Building Society calls on my behalf to
eak / to you on this subject on Thursday evening. People who / have had
nilar problems have taken advantage of our help / toward solving their
fficulties, but we cannot help you if / you have not told us of your
fficulty. In that / case we can only assume you have no wish to / pay and
rn you of our policy to repossess.   (*139 words*)

Practical dictation

Extract from an annual report to shareholders

This report describes what your company has achieved over the / last
year, and we hope you will find it informative. / The profits rose by 10
per cent this year thanks / to the activities of the research and

development team and / our well-motivated workforce. We gave a more effective service / to our customers with no increase in tariffs. W hope / the dividend we have given to you will represent a / good incentive to keep your loyal support. The remaining one / third of o profits will be given over to reserves.   (*90 words*)

2 Building society letter regarding a mortgage advanc

Dear Sir

I refer to your telephone call of yesterday / afternoon and am able t approve releasing half of the / mortgage advance in principle, provide that the valuer's report on / the building proves to be satisfactory ar that all the / Society's terms, of which you were told, have been observed. / However, I would prefer that you and your wife come / see me in private at 3 pm next / Wednesday afternoon to finalise t rough draft of the advance / form. Please advise me if this arrangeme proves difficult for / you.

Yours faithfully   (*93 words*)

3 Extract from an article on the 'Black Economy'

In brief, the 'Black Economy' is the name given to / a number of activities which are done in private for / cash and the profits derive out of these are undeclared / to the taxman. Those driven to these activities are in / danger of tough measures from the Government wh proof is / provided of their activities. The grave measures taken again them / serve to be effective in preventing others from doing the / sam Tax rules should be observed by everyone and not / to do so means t tax burden on those providing / the taxes is very heavy.   (*95 word*)

Theory check

1	.... above		6	.... divide
2	.... overdraft		7	.... photographic
3	.... perfect		8	.... Thursday afternoon
4	.... province		9	.... alternative
5	.... drives		10	.... photography

Reading and writing practice – 1

It is our intention to press for the motion to be carried at the morning session tomorrow.

Following intensive revision with the teacher in class, they found the examination quite easy.

Attention paid to the list of cancellations will enable you to make a flight reservation to a different destination.

We should commission our Sales Promotion Department to organise a fashion show and the money charged for admission will be given to a worthy cause.

It is necessary to seek professional advice when building an extension to your home.

Reading and writing practice – 2

On discussion with the Chairman of the company, it was decided to offer the promotion to the junior in the reception office.

The resolution to strike caused much aggression among the staff.

The Section Head had no hesitation in granting permission for the holiday bonus to be paid.

The bank official had no recollection that the transaction had been approved and details entered in the data bank.

According to the specification, the location of the site is opposite the station.

Reading and writing practice – 3

To mark the occasion of the company's expansion into the European market, a presentation was made to the Chairman.

2   A large section of the local population signed the petition against t**
    provision of a petrol station on the road.
3   The police officer cautioned the protest group and said that no actio
    would be taken on this occasion.
4   On receipt of your application for a change of occupation, we shall
    approach the local education department to ascertain whether they
    have any vacancies in their other sections.
5   In addition to the usual games at our annual children's party, we ha
    booked the services of a local magician.

Reading and writing practice – 4

1   The hire purchase company took possession of the property becaus
    of the arrears in payments owed to them.
2   The Musicians' Union applied for dispensation from taxation since t**
    proceeds of the Pop Festival would be donated to charity.
3   The magistrate's decision to free the defendant caused a sensation i
    the court.
4   A desperate housing situation has been created within the city becau
    of a lack of money.
5   It is usually found that staff who take advantage of private tuition wh
    studying for professional examinations make better progress.

Reading and writing practice – 5

1   In our opinion we would be extremely foolish not to take advantage
    the bank's Customer Advisory Service.
2   The social economy of this country has changed drastically during t**
    past two decades.
3   The decision to limit the amount of fish taken from the sea will ensure
    plentiful supply for the next generation.
4   We are waiting for our surveyor to finish his inspection and produce h
    report before we can put the work in hand.
5   In view of his valuable service over the years, it was decided to mak
    him an Associate Member of the Association.

he investigation was productive and sufficient to prove that the / iformation had been given efficiently to the local representative of / your rganisation. It was his responsibility to pass on to / the Medical ssociation any objections he had received regarding the / lengthy aiting-lists for admission to the hospitals in our / area. I feel we should go) great lengths to / guard against these lists being made public. The roduction of / this information to the national press would give much itisfaction / to the opposition party.   (*84 words*)

Letter regarding a statement in the press

Dear Sir

Our attention has been called to the observations / you made in the national press on Monday regarding the / old railway station situated in our town. In your position / and with your education, you should be sure your information / is correct before making such a public statement.

The station / is a listed building and its upkeep is the responsibility / of a well-known national organisation. There are, at the / moment, several objections to the plans submitted detailing the proposed / alterations, but the organisation and the local authority are working / together to obtain planning permission to renovate this great building. /

Yours faithfully   (*102 words*)

Letter to a removal firm

Dear Sir

At the end of February I shall be / changing my present occupation for a position in the south. / It is my intention to arrange the removal of my / household effects during the first week of March. I have / in my possession a collection of rare silver, and great / care and attention must be taken with the packing and / loading of these valuable items.

I should be pleased if / your representative could call to assess the situation and give / me full information regarding the proposed removal. I shall also / need professional advice regarding insurance.

Yours faithfully   (*97 words*)

3 Memo to: Managing Director   From: Personnel Manager
Subject: John Taylor   Date: Today's

John Taylor, our Production Manager, has handed in his resignation / as he is joining an associate company of ours. He / has been studying for professional examinations at the local college / of education and has achieved excellent results.

On his own / admission he feels he has little chance of promotion in / our company, in view of the current financial climate.

John / is an excellent manager who accepts full responsibility for his / department and in my estimation would be a sad loss / to this firm. I should like to have a discussion / with you to see if an exception could be made / in his case.   (*103 words*)

Theory check

1 .... additional

2 .... appreciated

3 .... notification

4 .... educational

5 .... resolutions

6 .... auction

7 .... edition

8 .... musicians

9 .... sugar

10 .... dish

Compound consonants and the omission of consonants

Send a telex asking for a quotation for a quantity of a quarter of a million.

We will need a bilingual secretary quickly if they accept our quote.

The bank is fully acquainted with our financial state of affairs and is pressing us to quit now and go into liquidation.

Your linguistic abilities adequately meet our requirements but we would like you to acquire extra fluency in Japanese.

The questionnaire shows that the public require a high quality product and a quick sales service in response to their enquiries.

Reading and writing practice – 2

I emboldened the headings on impulse but I think you will agree that the end product is most impressive.

It is imperative that this campaign is successful. Do I need to make myself clearer?

The Chancellor is to visit our embassy on the 4th, so inform the ambassador immediately.

I am sorry to be the bearer of bad news; he has been found guilty of embezzlement — much to the embarrassment of the company.

The Chancellor says that imports are down and exports up so it will not be necessary for the Government to impose higher taxes on imported goods.

Reading and writing practice – 3

Ring the post office and enquire about special express postal services for overseas.

2 We will have to postpone the despatch of invitations to the Queen's Birthday banquet because of adjustments which have to be made to the list of guests of distinction.

3 I am tempted to do the mail shot now, based on the assumption that postal charges will rise before long.

4 It seems an analogue quartz was sent by mistake. Substitute one of the digital range and enclose some postage stamps to refund the customer's postal costs.

5 I am anxious that you take charge of the inquiry and investigate how the institution has failed to notice such a gross embezzlement of its funds.

Short form and phrasing practice

Dear Sirs

Over the past few years we have done / much business with you at Hi-tec Business Systems p / lc, and have been particularly impressed with the service / we have been given. However, over the past few months, / it seems it has been almost impossible to get the / particular delivery service from you which we have come to / expect. Last week we sent you a most important telex / asking for delivery as quickly as possible of one more / monitor as well as two more of the improved keyboards. / However, according to the Systems Manager, you have neglected to / deliver. If there is no general improvement over the next / few months and, in particular, if you do not take / this opportunity to send us what we require within the / next few days this is the last time you may / expect to hear from our Corporation. We will simply take / our business elsewhere.

Yours faithfully   *(155 words)*

Practical dictation

1 Letter regarding an inaccurate quotation

Dear Sir

I refer to your quotation dated 10 November / and believe there must be two mistakes in this. Firstly, / I only requested a quote for a quarter of the / equipment which appears on this quotation, but assume the quantity / discount of 15 per cent shown in the last line / still applies. Secondly, there is no mention of the additional / rollers which I enquired about. Please let me have the / amended quotation as quickly as possible.

Yours faithfully   *(78 words)*

Memo to: Secretarial Staff

From: Post room Supervisor

Subject: Addressing envelopes

Date: Today's

It is important that addresses are typed roughly midway down / and one third across the front of a standard envelope / . This leaves adequate room for the post room attendants to / add postage stamps or the post office the postmark. Postcodes / should be quoted at all times and occupy the last / line as requested by the post office. Mistakes should be / clearly corrected and requests for special postal services clearly stated. / All postal items must reach the post room by 4. / 30 pm as the postman calls at 5.30 / pm to take the postbags to the post office. / Please institute these requirements to avoid the wasteful use of / time and stationery which has occurred over the past year. /
(*120 words*)

Advertisement for a bilingual secretary

We are a young, go-ahead company about to embark / on a new sales campaign in the Far East. We / are anxious to appoint a bilingual secretary with a fluent / linguistic ability in a Far Eastern language *stroke* languages. We / are seeking a person with ambition who can quickly acquaint / himself *stroke* herself with our organisation and then institute changes / appropriate to this expansion. It is imperative that the successful / candidate has experience of modern business equipment and has acquired / secretarial skills of the highest quality (one hundred and twenty / *stroke* sixty). Please address all enquiries to Mr Peter White, / Sales Manager (Overseas Division), enclosing a stamped addressed envelope.   (*109 words*)

Theory check

.... question	**6**	.... imposition
.... multi-lingual	**7**	.... investigate
.... temporary	**8**	.... distinct
.... embezzler	**9**	.... fuller
.... language	**10**	.... implication

Doubling

Reading and writing practice – 1

1   After their holiday in France, my father, mother and sister returned to find their house had been broken into.
2   We prefer not to look further into the future than the remainder of this year.
3   Before the election the voters were sent another letter from each of the candidates.
4   Neither of the two exporters was able to fulfil the order by the date required.
5   Further to your letter of 16 April referring to order number 628, we fully intend to investigate the matter and will write to you again after we have spoken to our fitter.

Reading and writing practice – 2

1   Many washing powders claim to wash whiter but our powder is exceptional even in harder water.
2   The tutor prepared his talk on the subject of the structure of business.
3   The director authorised the purchase of five new typewriters to cater for the increased work load in the export sector.
4   It is a wonder the reader managed to finish the chapter as he appeared to squander his time making pictures on his blotter.
5   The helicopter rose into the air, its rotor blades scattering the leaves in all directions.

Reading and writing practice – 3

1   On a wintry day in December the temperature on the thermometer fell to minus three degrees Celsius.

The firm put in a tender for the supply of new tankers but did not get the order.

As he caught the cricket ball on the boundary, the fielder broke his little finger.

Although he tried hard to conquer his temper, the banker's anger got the better of him on that September day.

The lack of a seconder for the banker's proposition naturally rendered the whole matter null and void.

hort form and phrasing practice

ar Sirs

Thank you for your letter expressing your interest / in our new range of nderfully improved water heaters. You / may wonder how our heaters er from those of some / other manufacturers. Therefore we have pleasure enclosing a selection / of our publicity material in order that you may ly / appreciate the character of the improvements we have made. wever, / if you would rather see these heaters in operation, the / writer of s letter will be more than happy to / make arrangements for you to visit showroom. In there / you may carry out exhaustive tests, after which we nk / you will acknowledge that our products sent from there are / erything we claim. In other words, we are totally secure / in our wledge that the quality of our merchandise is / better than any other. We e to hear from you / in the near future.

Yours faithfully   (*146 words*)

ractical dictation

Newspaper report of a road traffic accident

On the afternoon of 14 September our reporter witnessed an / accident between a motor car and a tractor at the / junction of Central Avenue and Carpenter Close. The front screen / of the motor car was shattered, the glass splintered and / scattered in all directions. It is a wonder that neither / driver was seriously hurt and that many other people were / not injured. The tractor driver maintained that he had not / seen the motor car's indicator flashing because of the bushes / on the border of the central reservation. As a matter / of fact, at other times this accident could have been / more serious. Among other things, an inspector has been appointed / in order to see if there is any other way / of handling traffic at this particular intersection.

(*127 words*)

2 Business letter

Dear Sirs

Thank you for your letter of 10 December / in which you ask for
extension of time for / payment of the account which we rendered
the end / of September. We acknowledge that you have been going
through / a difficult period but the fact of the matter is / that you d
enter into an agreement with us to / pay a fixed sum each month for tl
refrigerators with / which you have been supplied. This you have fail
to / do. Therefore our directors are afraid that, rather than wait / al
longer, we may be forced to adopt stronger measures / unless you re
not later than the end of this / month. We are no longer willing to pl
the role / of creditor.

Yours faithfully   (*124 words*)

3 Circular

Dear Householder

Does the thought of decorating your home make / you shudder?
so, you may be interested to know / that I am shortly moving my
builder's, painter's and decorator's / business to your area and I shou
be pleased to / tender for any such work from major structural
alterations to / merely decorating the lumber-room. A central featu
of the / better service I offer is the wide range of materials / with whi
I work, from the simple treatment of natural / timber to techniques
the most advanced character. If you / require further particulars or
you think there is anything / I could help you with in future, just get i
touch with my company, Henderson and Walters, at the address /
given at the head of this letter.

Yours truly (*129 words*)

Theory check

1	order	6	adventure
2	letter	7	holder
3	leather	8	dictator
4	ponder	9	hunger
5	sombre	10	going there

Prefixes, suffixes and word endings

Prefixes, suffixes and word endings

Reading and writing practice – 1

The Company Secretary will consider the contents of the confidential report.

The computer exhibition was held at the conference centre last year.

The company will reconsider its decision to discontinue making components following adverse comments from buyers.

The committee recommended that accompanied tours abroad for senior directors should be introduced.

The hotel accommodation was very comfortable and had magnificent views.

Reading and writing practice – 2

The self-contained apartment was located near to public transport.

In the self-interest of our company it is necessary for the transmission of the gas to take place as soon as possible.

It is self-evident that his transfer to our southern branch would be to our advantage.

It is unnecessary to telephone her. She made arrangements to come to the office today to instruct us regarding her inheritance.

Unknown to the laboratory staff, the instruments were illegal.

Reading and writing practice – 3

The shipping could enter the harbour only in the mornings.

The announcement outlined the interesting achievements of the company and stated that the building work commencement date would soon be available.

The staff at the experimental laboratory buildings were requesting more security because they considered it necessary.

4 The ownership of the club passed to the membership and included the use of all facilities.

5 It was thoughtlessness on his part which caused hardship to them and ruined the friendship.

Reading and writing practice – 4

1 There is a possibility that the filing system will be changed from a chronological to an alphabetical one.

2 The majority wanted the chairman to stay, but a minority was calling for his resignation.

3 The personnel officer was informed that physically the workman was sound but that he appeared to be psychologically disturbed.

4 He went backwards and forwards between the shipyard and the brickyard to deliver materials.

5 It is fairly easy to obtain the cases with reasonable promptness, and they are cheaply priced and particularly useful for storage purposes.

Short form and phrasing practice

The Government is concerned about the marked rise in persuasive / advertisements. Although commercially profitable, it is known that when goods / are advertised on a regular basis, it is probable that / some individuals are tempted to buy, even though they do / not have sufficient income. As skilful marketing increases the probability / of people wanting to own the article, the prospects of / selling become greatly increased. From the commercial point of view, / to advertise regularly probably results in more demand for goods. / In the circumstances, individual advertisements are presented in an attractive / and instructive manner. As the rôle of advertising is so / important, the Government feels that more guidelines would probably be / welcome to govern the circumstances in which certain advertisements are / presented. Members of a special committee are individually being asked / to give their comments with a view to instructions being / drawn up. Despite the fact that advertising is an important / influence on many people, the feelings of the committee must be partially governed by the fact that the advertising world / is a major employer. (*174 words*)

Letter regarding a computer club

Dear Mr Compton

Thank you for requesting details of our / Computer Club. Further to our telephone conversation, I enclose information / on our activities for your consideration. Membership fees are paid / on a yearly basis and the advantages of joining our / club are many. Members meet regularly twice a week, and / we invite you to come to our meeting on Wednesday / next so that you can see the club in action / for yourself and meet our members.

We invite speakers from / industry, universities and colleges to talk to us and we / arrange visits to see computer networks. We obtain reduced entry / rates to the major computer exhibitions and arrange transport. Most / of the large computer software agents allow a generous discount / to club members.

Once a year we arrange a visit / abroad to a place of interest for our members, and / this year the visit is to America to see Silicon / Valley.

Yours sincerely   (*153 words*)

Memorandum from Marketing Director to all sales staff

I am pleased to announce that our marketing campaign is / now ready to commence next week.

As you already know, / desk and field research indicate that there should be a / considerable market for our goods in our three major target / areas. Field research indicated that only a small minority of / the inhabitants did not use our type of products and / random sampling leads us to believe that our goods will / be purchased. Trial samples used in selected households have proved / to be successful.

The local shops have made arrangements for / our specialist sales teams to display our goods for one / week. We are, therefore, ordering sufficient supplies, and further consignments / are available.

I am compelled to say that our new / product has stiff competition, but I am confident that skilful / marketing will allow us to capture a large share of / the market.   (*142 words*)

Memorandum from Personnel Manager to Training Manager

I have received a letter from the Principal of the / local college of further education asking us if we are / interested in talking to their

students who are about to / complete their courses this year. You w
remember that last / year my visit was extremely useful, resulting in tl
recruitment / of several new employees, and I am confident that you
talk this year will be equally valuable. I suggest that / you contact tl
Principal at once to arrange a suitable / date.

You will find it helpful to take our new / recruitment video whic
explains in detail our interview procedures and / the reasoning behii
our psychological testing.

During the question and / answer period after your talk students
usually ask about conditions / of service and rates of pay, so please
ensure that / you have up-to-date figures for all grades.   (*139 word*

Theory check

1 .... community

2 .... uncommon

3 .... transportation

4 .... illegible

5 .... running

6 .... desirability

7 .... self-satisfied

8 .... connected

9 .... accommodate

10 .... inhospitable